Hansha
Notebook
(with Hansha templates)

© **Alta H Haffner 2024**

ISBN: 978-0-7961-6582-4

ALL RIGHTS RESERVED

alta@sakurabookpublishing.com

Hansha

Embark on a poetic journey beyond the ordinary with "Hansha" Mastering the Art of Reflective Verses," the definitive guide to Hansha, a poetry form created by poet Alta H. Haffner. This exquisite template book is designed to guide you through the process of crafting your reflective verses.

Hansha's structure invites introspection and exploration, making it a perfect medium for expressing the dualities of the human experience.

As you progress through the book, you'll gain the confidence to experiment with different moods and themes, in the composition of your own Hansha poems. The pages are graced with ample space for drafting and revising, with examples of Hansha poems written by Alta H Haffner.

Mastering the Art of *HANSHA* will guide you to this mesmerizing form of poetic expression, and watch as your words become a mirror to your soul.

HANSHA ~ Han-shaa
5~5~7   5~5~7

#hanshabyaltahhaffner

A form of Haiku created by South African haikuist Alta H Haffner.

With the focus on deep reflection and introspection within the context of the brevity and nature-inspired haiku structure. Poems within this form will invite readers to contemplate and find meaning in the natural world and their own inner thoughts and emotions. It's a form that captures the essence of what a haiku strives to achieve: a moment of reflection and connection with the beauty of the world around us.

Syllable count - 5-5-7- but allows the freedom for less but not more syllables.
First line 5 syllables
Second line 5 syllables and must consist of either nature or meditation.
Third line 7 syllables and must include a moment of reflection.

tranquil rivers flow
sakura blooming
guided steps to peacefulness ~Alta H Haffner

endless waves embrace
ocean calls my soul
soft whispers of acceptance ~Alta H Haffner

Hansha" 反射 ~ REFLECTION

About Alta H Haffner

Alta H. Haffner is a Haiku poet whose work captures the essence of precious, fleeting moments with simplicity and depth. Born with a deep appreciation for the beauty of brevity, Alta's Haiku poems reflect her keen observation of nature and her ability to evoke emotions in just a few short lines.

Drawing inspiration from the ever-changing seasons, the delicate balance of the natural world, and the quiet whispers of every new dawn, Alta's Haiku poems invite readers to slow down, pause, and appreciate the present moment. With a handful of syllables, she allows her readers to contemplate.

Through her Haiku poetry, Alta H. Haffner reminds us of the beauty that can be found in simplicity, the power of mindfulness, and the importance of being fully present in each moment.

More books by Alta H Haffner

river of heaven
rice sparrow in flight
fog clearing at amber dusk

droplets of spring rain
cherry blossom breeze
a lingering chill morning

autumns voice calling
warmth of a fireplace
the milky way greets the moon

the winds embrace

orchid petals cried

love after the storm settled

rainbow colored sky
beautiful summer rain pour
tears fall as I miss you

soft voice of the reeds

companion at dawn

in silence my soul finds peace

a starry night glow

crickets in duet

whispers of tranquility

peaceful and calm noon

azure clouds floating

rejuvenating my soul

breathtaking morning
sleepy waves swaying
a gentle kiss of sunlight

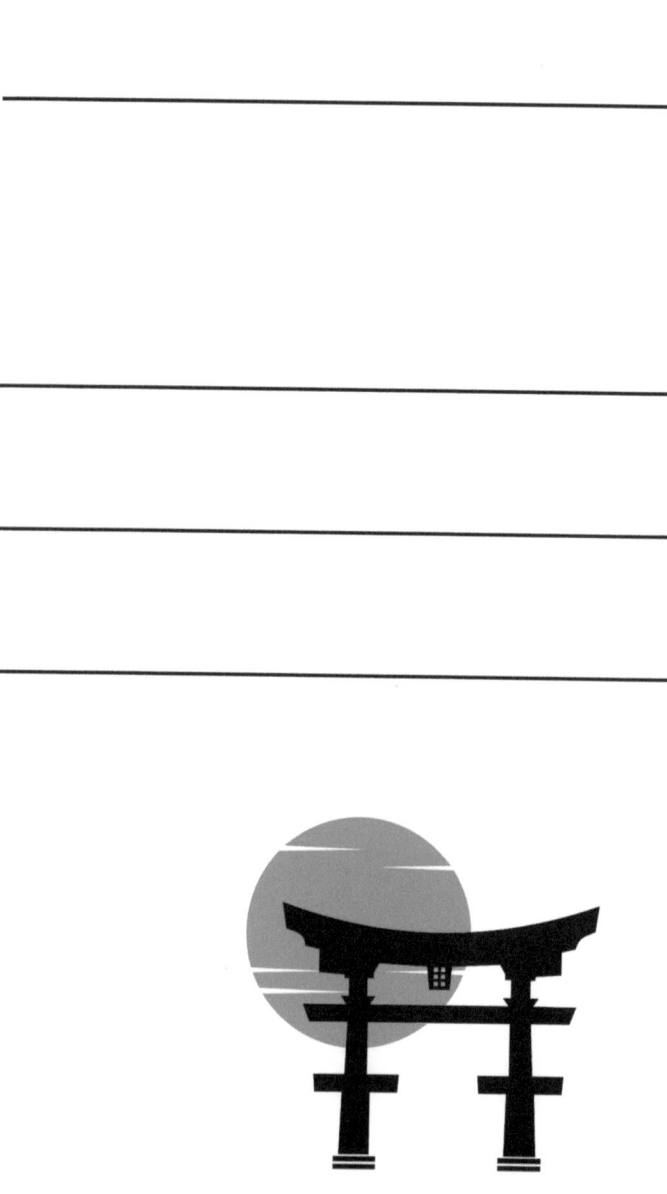

awake at dawns light

with pure intentions

reflect the magic within

golden hue sunset

awake inner peace

embrace pure tranquility

heavenly rainbow
wisteria bloom
the sound of a waterfall

the north wind rising

steaming pumpkin pie

a sleepy snow-capped mountain

autumn sky deepens
patches of green fade
lonely dance of fallen leaves

_____

_____

_____

_____

_____

_____

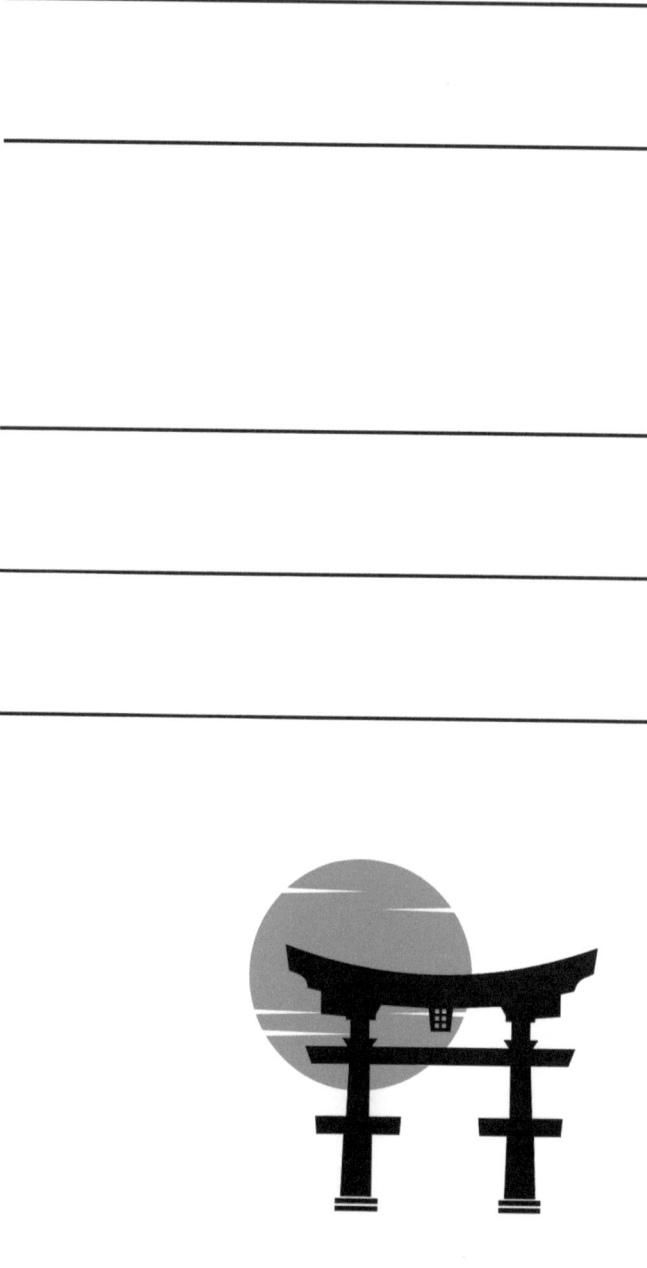

our breathless moments
hold onto my moon
glitzy diamond sky canvas

shadows of the moon
the stars shining bright
rests in a cold wishing well

peaceful calming waves
reflecting within
tranquility of deep blue

bat in flight to moon
peaceful starry night
an old owl catching a nap

bright lights in gloaming

mesmerizing glow

ocean inhaling the moon

syllables blooming
counting at first light
thoughts change from winter to spring

a thunderous storm
sun shining again
the rainbow colors sparkle

whisper silently
chanting at dawns light
spiritual peace and love

calmness of the mind

darkest clouds settling

endless emotions spinning

a golden sunrise

perfect harmony

morning breeze summers fragrance

the late moon shines bright

awaiting dawns light

shadows of all withered trees

contemplative thoughts
picturesque nature
tiny buds blooming daily

tranquility held

endless peace and hope

peace in the chaos around

blissful morning sun
accepting my path
embracing soft white petals

from grey to amber

a gentle goodnight

moonlight kisses lingering

forlorn memories
an eagle in flight
breezy cold winters night

in my darkest night
gaze at shooting stars
bright Northern star guiding me

flowers in Spring bloom
all new beginnings
embracing the icy winds

the sun settling slow
a gentle soft breeze
dusky skies and peacefulness

nature in summer
carpet of colors
butterflies dance on petals

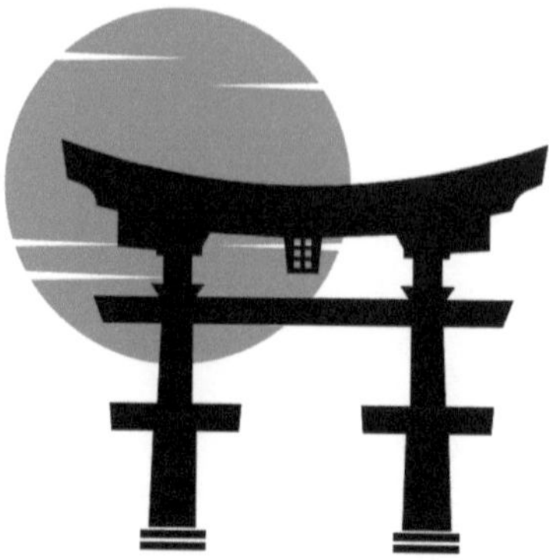

the calm ocean waves

a crab runs on sand

reflect amber twilight glow

soft whispering winds
dew drizzled petals
a cold spring morning breaks

foggy forest walk
woodpecker looks on
icicle covered brown leaves

take a break dear heart

a new dawns greeting

to appreciate soul friends

spring is in the air
lovers say I do
the smell of the first rainspout

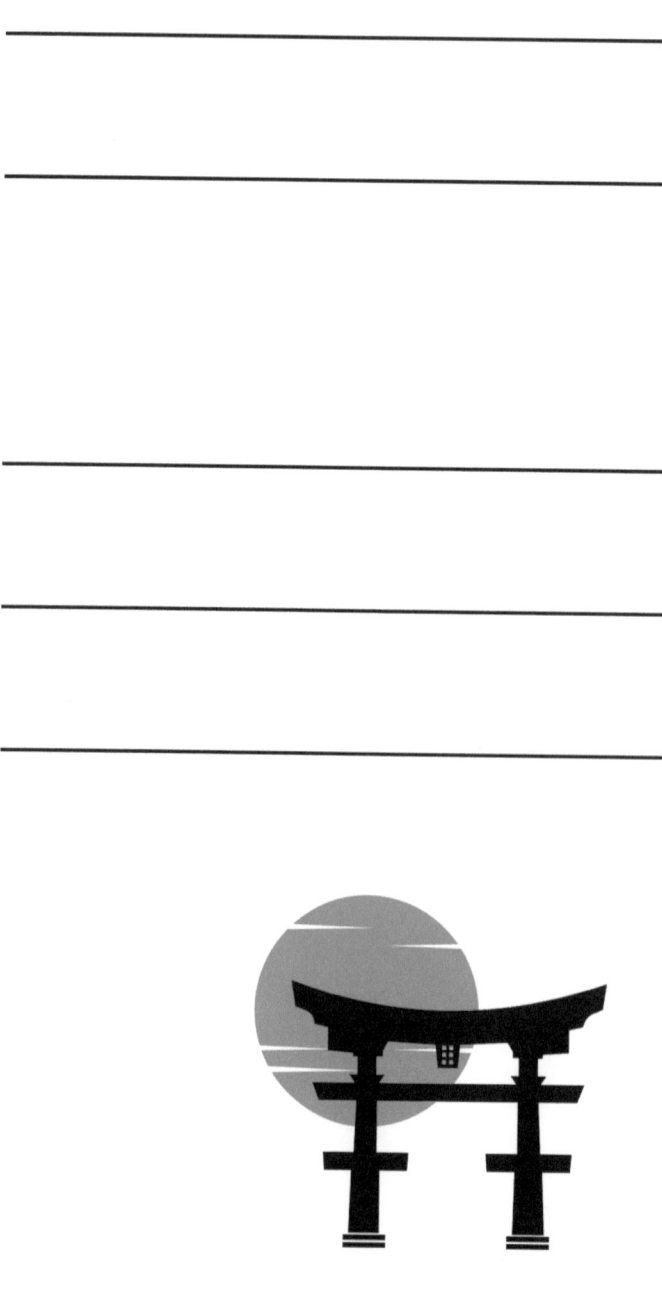

soft blue horizon

foamy waves dancing

memories fade into the wind

encompass fully

peace and joyfulness

under a starry sky glow

glistening droplets

silence between stars

petals nurtured with nature

Inhale Sakura

calming the chaos

petals blooming in delight

brightest morning sun
sweet scent of Jasmine
birds nestled between branches

a Sakura path
soaking up nature
the beauty of a new Spring

the yellow orchid

sleepy petals rest

in full bloom of the shadow

morning misty dance

sun beaming brightly

color canvas of nature

mirrored reflections

breathtaking beauty

puffy clouds in horizon

go find your rainbow

inhale the moment

maybe no pot of gold yet

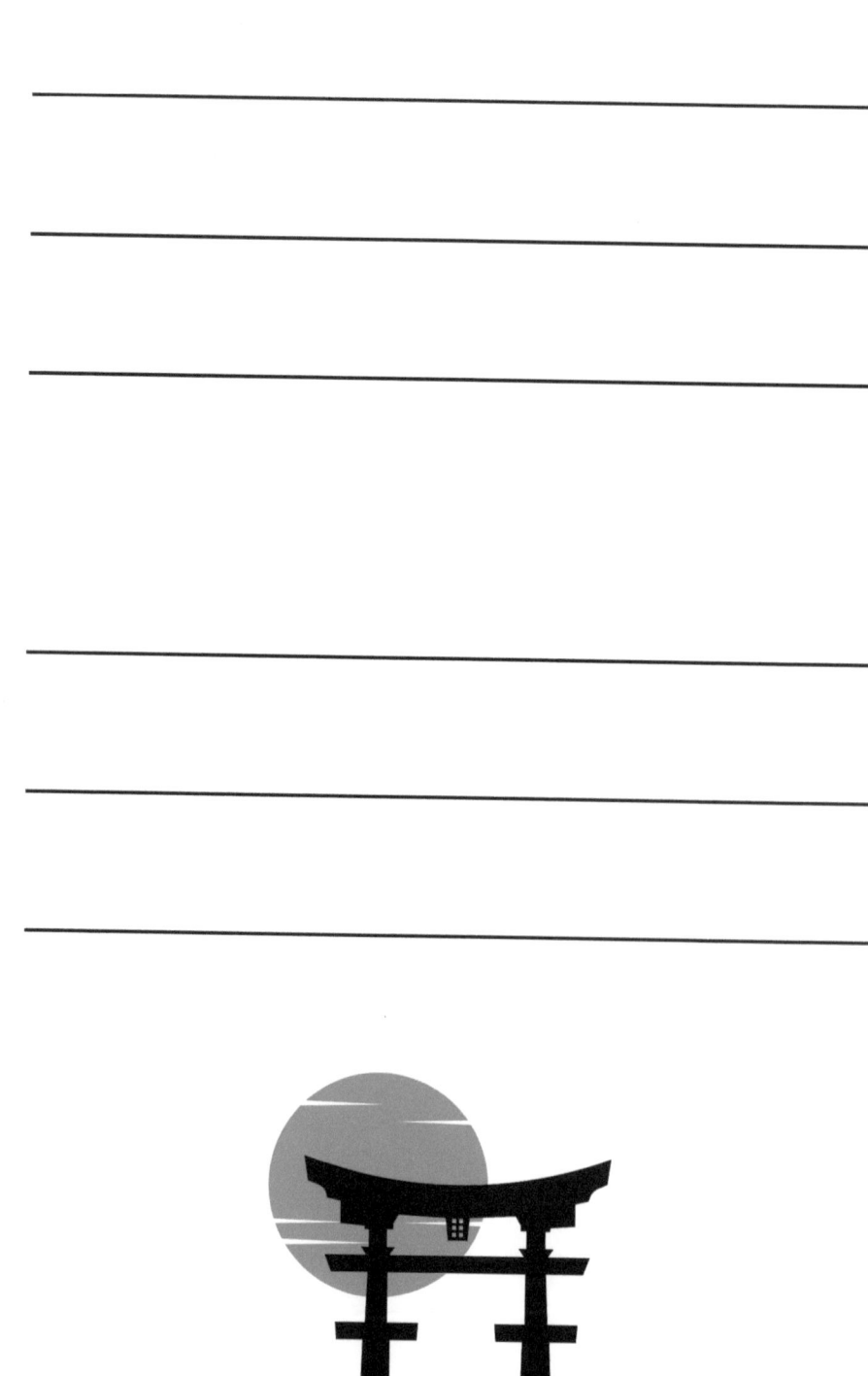

an amber sunset

breathe in the magic

in the midst of a snowfall

dandelion gift

it may just come true

make your craziest wishes

tranquility felt

to just breathe today

allowing your inner peace

morning brevity
a rainfall at noon
spectacular view behold

dancing in the breeze

petals opening

a colorful butterfly

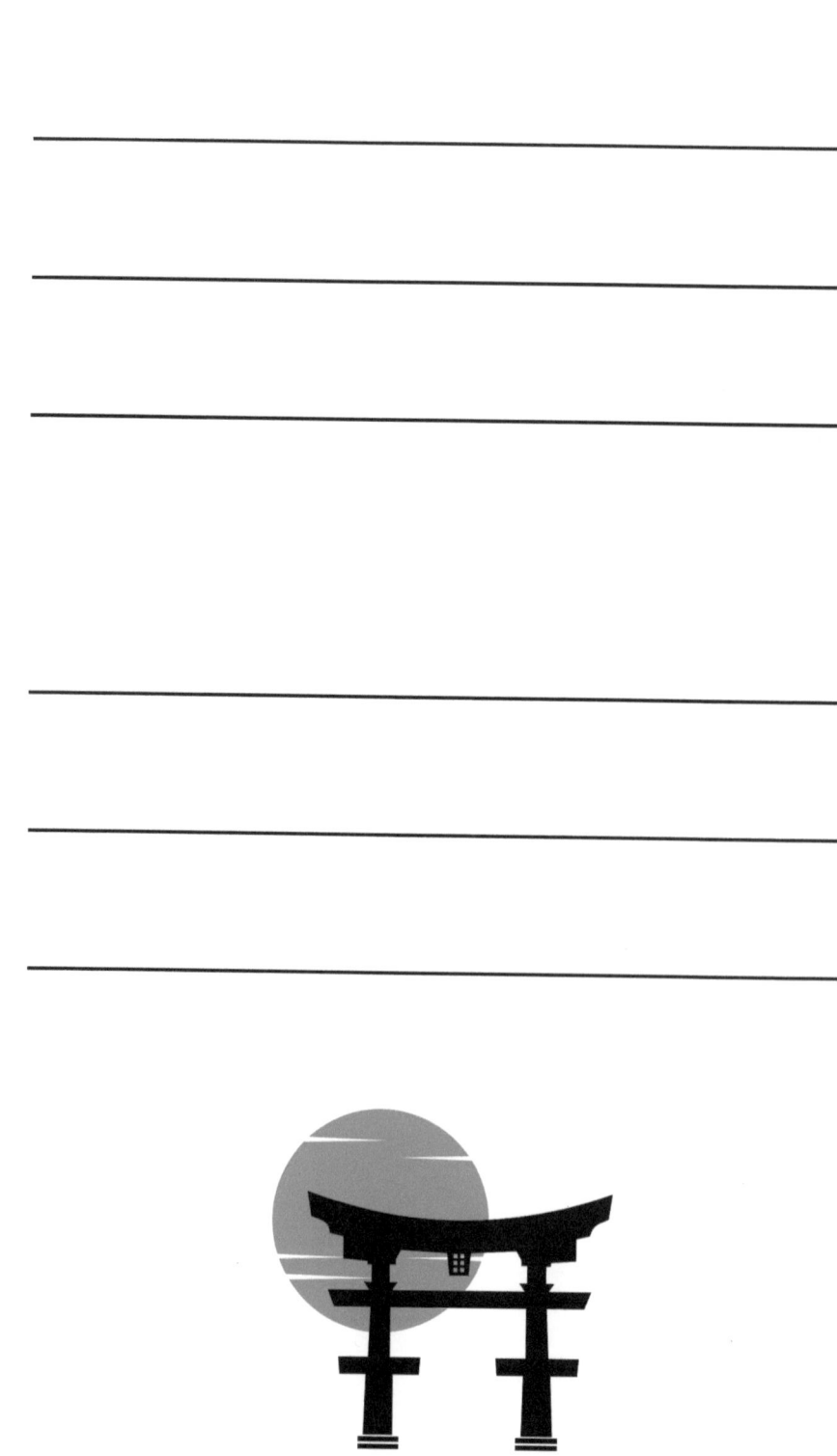

the morning sea waves

a seagull posing

covering shiny seashells

sun-kissed ocean waves

scattered memories

a glorious daybreak glow

scattered memories

emotions trembling

inhaling the oceans breath

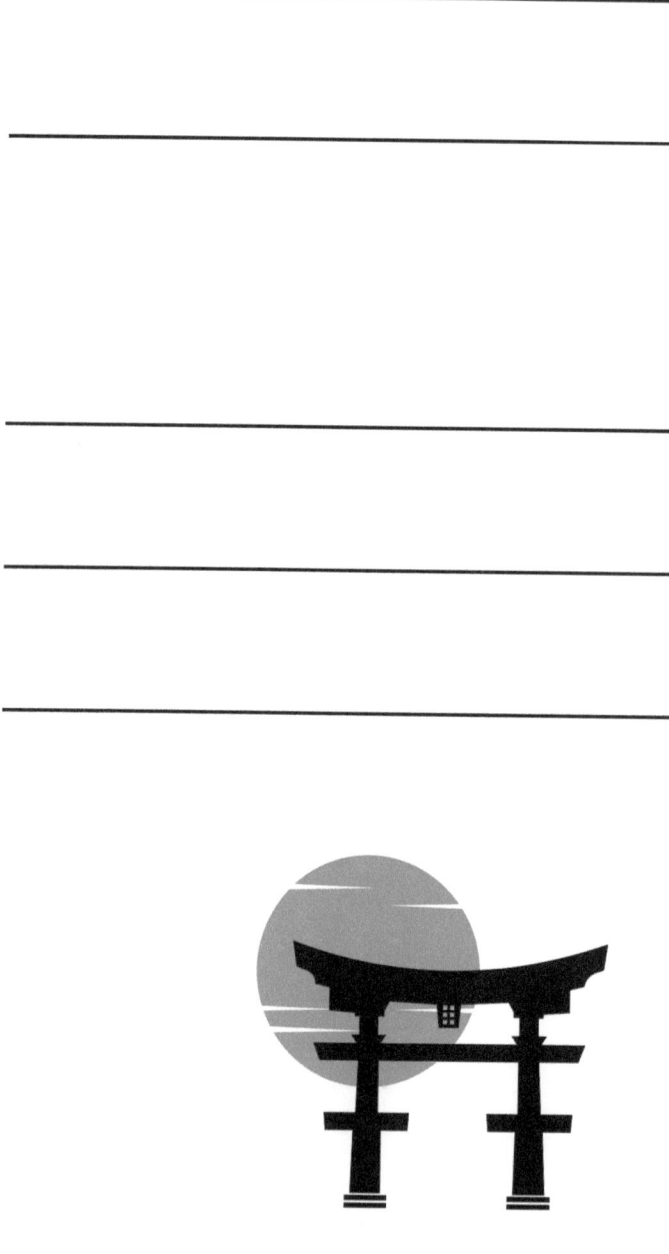

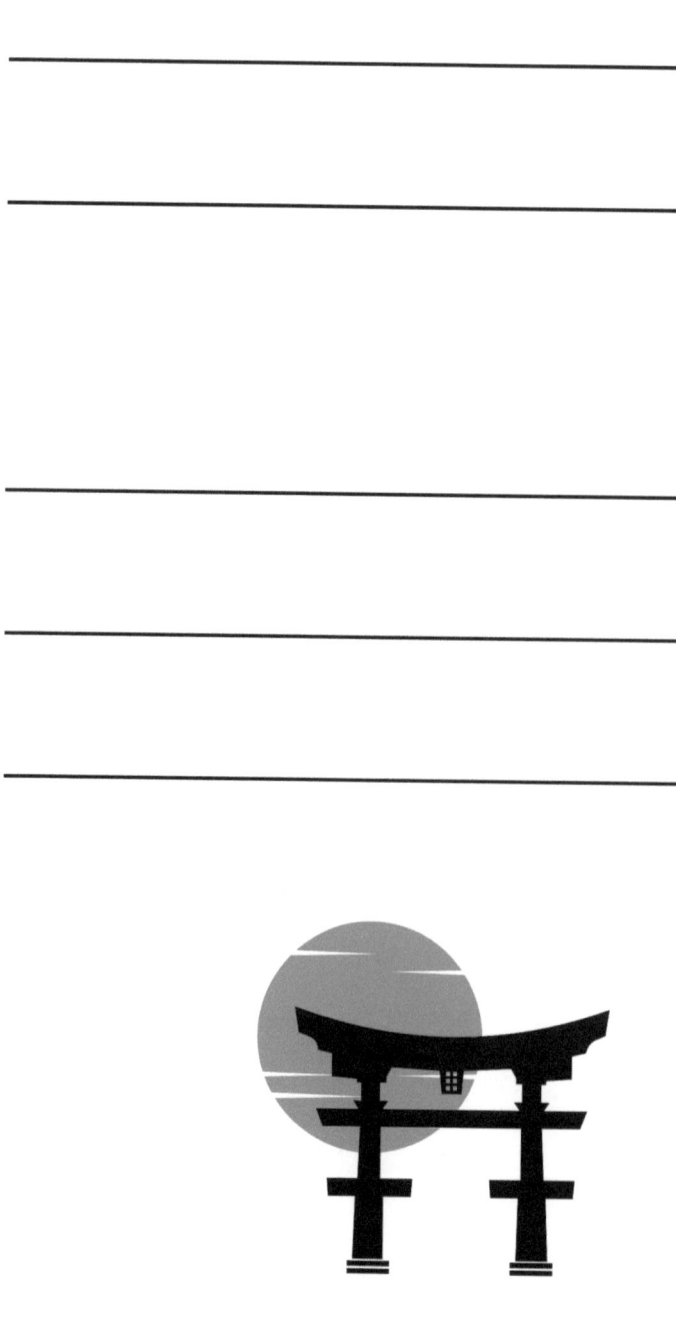

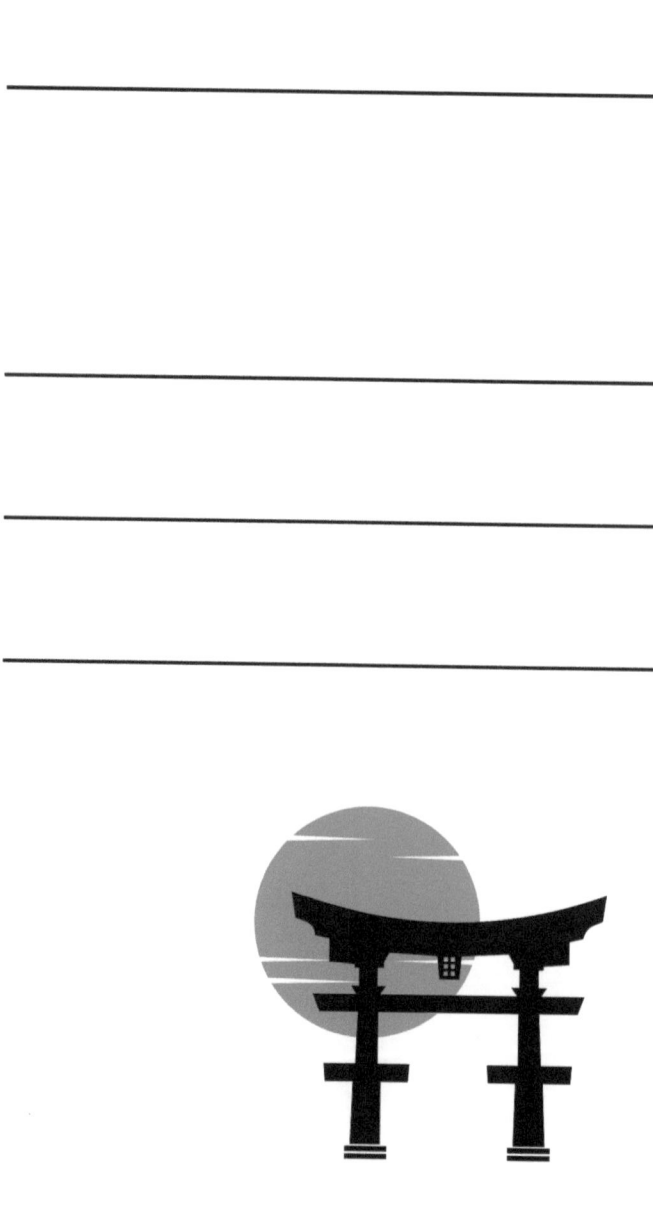

_____

_____

_____

_____

_____

_____

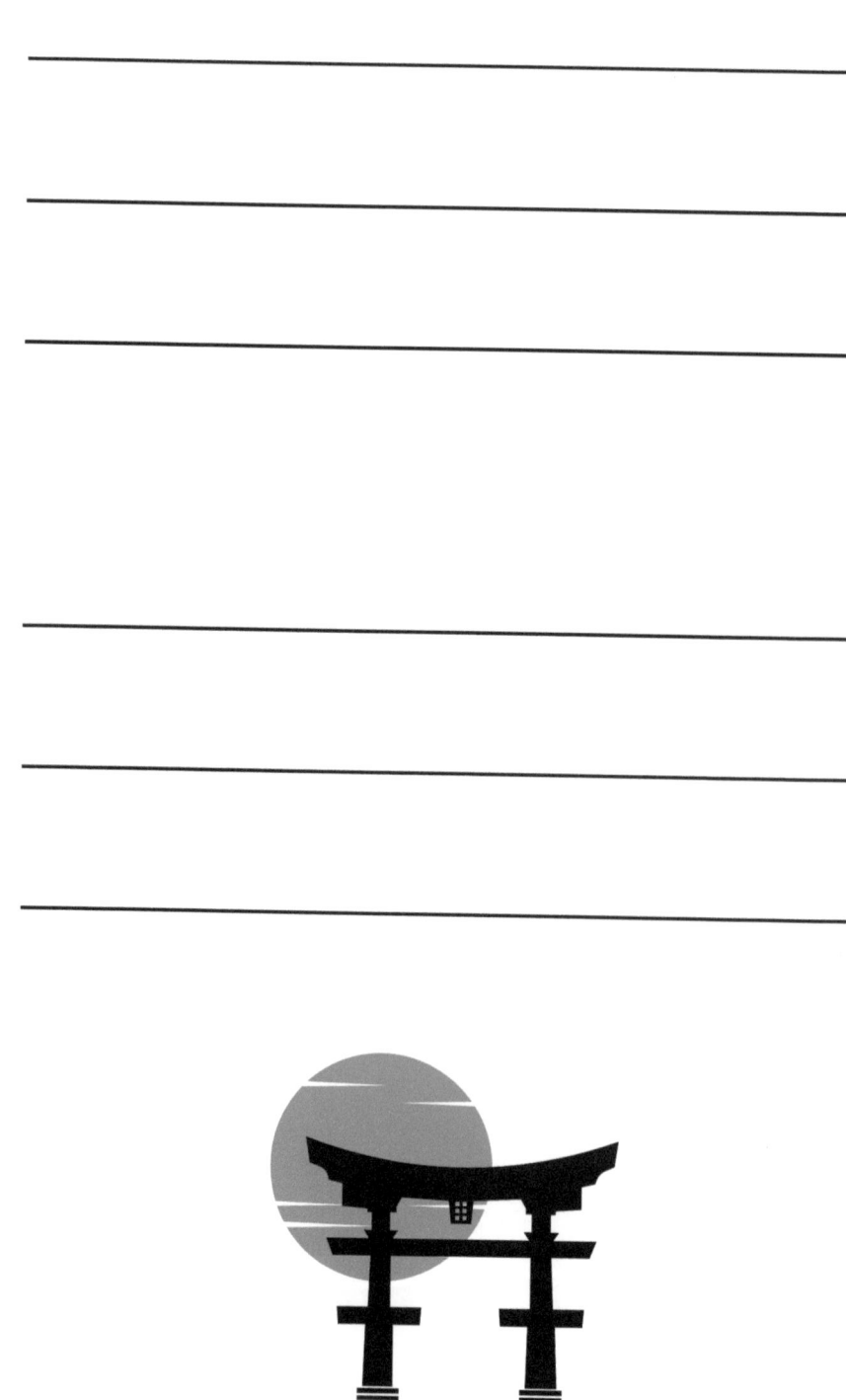

_____

_____

_____

_____

_____

_____

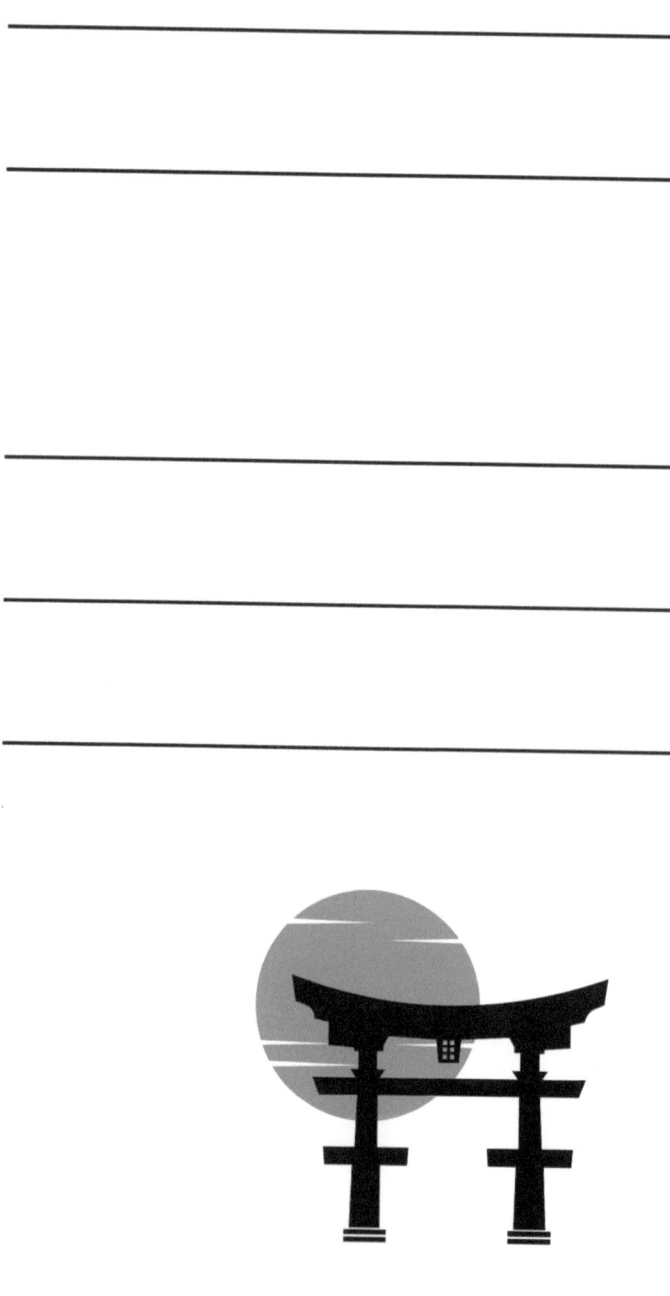

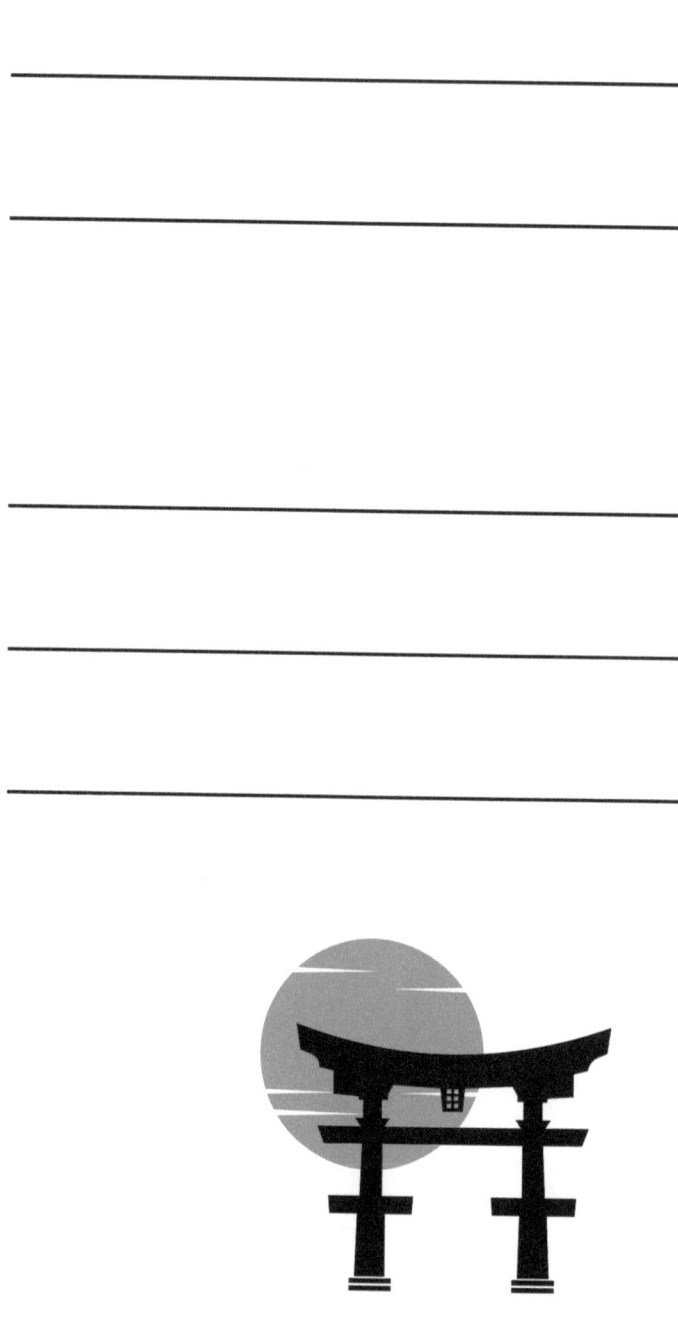

www.ingramcontent.com/pod-product-compliance
Lightning Source LLC
Chambersburg PA
CBHW042044290426
44109CB00001B/21